A GUIDE TO Book Printing

AND SELF-PUBLISHING

GORHAM PRINTING

A GREAT LOOK FOR YOUR SHORT-RUN BOOK

PRINTED AND PUBLISHED BY GORHAM PRINTING 2010

We are dedicated to making your book the best it can be. This guide will introduce you to the necessary preparations, technical printing details and key design decisions required for a successful transformation of your manuscript into a book.

We are a Pacific Northwest book printer specializing in the design and printing of self-published books. Our forté is the ability to print books in short print runs—from 25 to 3,000 copies—and in doing so, create a great look for your short-run book. Our shelves are filled with examples of our work, including fiction, non-fiction, religious, spiritual, historical, self-help, memoirs, manuals, how-to guides, genealogies, family histories, adventure, and more!

First-time writers as well as veteran authors have come to depend upon our hallmark qualities: careful attention to detail, customized design work, top-notch printing skills, and true, one-on-one, personal service. Just as you take pride as an author, we take pride in the books we print.

If you have any questions, concerns, or wish to have a price quote for your book project, don't hesitate to contact us. We look forward to hearing from you!

Visit us online
www.gorhamprinting.com

email us
info@gorhamprinting.com

call us
(800) 837-0970 or
(360) 623-1323

fax us
(360) 623-1325

mail us
3718 Mahoney Drive
Centralia, WA 98531

hours (Pacific Time)
8:00 - 4:30
Monday - Friday

Contents

Decisions
Affecting Cost

Decisions, Decisions...

Quantity and Cost

One of the first questions we hear is, "How much will it cost to print my book?" The answer depends largely on how many copies you want. In general, the more copies printed, the less each one costs. Setup expenses are the same whether we print twenty-five books or thousands; therefore if the cost of setup is spread over many books, the cost per book will be lower.

What size should it be?

Almost any size is possible up to 8½ x 11, but standard sizes are more efficient and less expensive. Our standard sizes are 5¼ x 8¼, 5½ x 8½, 6 x 9, 8¼ x 10¾ and 8½ x 11. These sizes are the most economical since they minimize paper waste.

To get the most for your money, keep your book to a standard trim size. For example, a 7 x 9 book (rather than a 6 x 9), will be priced at the 8½ x 11 size and trimmed down to 7 x 9.

The size of your book is sometimes dependent on its subject matter. 5½ x 8½ or 6 x 9 are the sizes most often used. A short column width makes the book very readable, easy to handle, ship and display.

A 6 x 9 book offers more space for photos, but for books with many photos, maps or illustrations, 8¼ x 10¾ (digital) or 8½ x 11 (offset) is a better size.

Note: If printed offset, your book will have 16–page signatures, so your total page count needs to be divisible by 16.

What kind of paper is used for the text?

Our "house sheet" is 60# white Weyerhaeuser Husky Offset for text, ordered in large quantities, resulting in savings for you. For offset books, we can also special-order other colors and weights upon request.

What kind of paper is used for the cover?

For softcover books we use white 10 point C1S, which is a heavy weight stock coated on one side (C1S). 12 point C1S is also available at additional cost. If the book is hardcover, the cover can be foil stamped or printed.

Prices

Refer to the price lists starting on page 23 to determine the cost of your book project.

Are we a publisher?

No. We design and produce your book. You are the publisher.

How is the cover protected?

The covers are film laminated. This protects the ink from scuffing and can give the book either a glossy or matte finish.

What about book design?

With designers on staff you are able to work one-on-one with the person designing your cover or text pages (see pages 10-15). Alternatively, you can provide your text and cover ready to print (see pages 16-17).

Bleeds

If you are planning a book with bleeds, it would be best to contact us first to see if it is feasible. Some restrictions due to size and other factors may make the project cost prohibitive.

How do you print digitally?

We use high speed toner-based black-and-white and color printers. Interior pages are usually printed on 60# white stock.

How do you print offset?

We use a perfector press capable of printing both sides of the sheet in one pass. For a 6x9 book we print on a 25x19 sheet, creating a 16–page signature.

What about photos?

We can print black-and-white photos using either offset or digital printing. Color photos are printed digitally. The quality of black-and-white photos printed offset is typically better than those printed digitally.

Are we a Print on Demand (POD) Printer?

No, most POD printers are set up to print one book at a time. Our minimum quantity is 25 books, however the cost per book is considerably less than printing one at a time.

What about special papers?

In most cases, special papers are limited to offset printing. A wider range of weights, colors and textures is available for offset printing than for digital printing. We do not use coated paper for perfect bound books, as the glue tends to adhere to the coating, rather than the fibers of the paper.

How do you print covers?

Digitally printed full-color covers are cost effective up to about 1,300 covers. Higher quantities are printed offset. For both digital and offset, we use a 10-point cover stock with gloss film lamination.

Matte lamination is also available, but is much more susceptible to scratches, scuffs and fingerprints than gloss lamination.

We Design
or You Design

If We Custom Design Your Cover

How does a great cover concept happen? Factors such as visual appeal, the audience for the book, color and font usage should be considered. In addition to conceptualizing the cover, a designer must have the technical skills to put those ideas into print. That's where we come in. At Gorham Printing, years of experience, expertise, and the right tools enable our designers to give your book a professional edge and enhance the salability of your book. Your cost for a complete custom cover design is $400.00.

Our proven approach will give you:

- **Collaboration.** After a discussion with you and reviewing your text, we will use our creative approach to imagery and layout in developing front cover ideas. We then email you the cover ideas for review. Your choice is then fine-tuned to a final unique design.

- **Cover image.** We can obtain a professional stock image from literally millions of choices that will perfectly compliment your cover. Or, we would be happy to use an image that you provide.

- **Printed color cover proof.** Once a front cover design has been established, the spine and back will be designed, and a printed proof will be sent to you.

- **Great communication.** We are easy to contact via email or phone. Your designer will work one-on-one with you throughout the design process. Further, your designer will oversee production, which is done here in our plant.

- **Files for marketing.** Graphic files of your cover design will also be available to you for use in print or online.

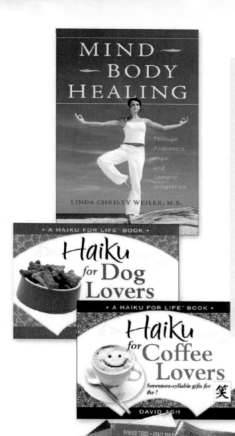

On our website

We Design It Section—
Visit this section to view
samples of our cover and
text design.

Information Section—Visit this
section to get specific Custom Design
information and instructions such as:

- **Book Cover Back Details**—
  All the information you need to
  formulate a back cover that sells.

- **Shipping Details**—Box count,
  weight and size.

If We Custom Design Your Text

Investing in good quality text design will make your book more readable and professional, resulting in more notice from booksellers, readers and publishers. Text layout is a subtle design process involving more than justifying margins and picking a typeface. With our design experience and knowledge of book design software we can handle the many technical details, and make your book look great in the process!

Custom Text Design Prices	
Sizes up to 6x9	$2.25 per page
8¼x10¾ or 8½x11	$3.50 per page
Template Prices	$100 for first 64 pages, $.90 per page after

What will the page count be?

When we design your book, the number of pages will probably change from your original manuscript. See the formulas below to calculate an estimated page count.

Don't forget to consider the space taken by photos or drawings. Also allow additional pages for front matter and back matter.

Total word count ÷ Words per page = approx. page count

Book size	Words per page
5¼x8¼ or 5½x8½	300
6x9	350
8¼x10¾ or 8½x11	400

How do we design your text?

To design your text pages, we will need a text file of the book to import into Adobe InDesign. Some programs we can accept:

- Microsoft Word (any version)
- Wordperfect
- Microsoft Publisher

It is best to have the whole book saved as a single file, with no graphics or photos included—we will add those later.

Design Process

After you send us your original text files, we will scan or place any images and design a text layout of your whole book. Then we mail you a printed proof. (For complex layouts, we will email a few sample pages first.)

You then mark the text with any final changes for us to make. Editorial corrections can be made at an hourly rate after the files come to us, but we recommend you submit your files in a final edited form to avoid additional charges.

On our website

We Design It Section— Visit this section to view samples of our cover and text design.

Information Section—Visit this section to get specific Custom Design information and instructions such as:

- **Special Characters**—Ever wondered how to make a copyright symbol or trademark? It's right here.

- **Indexing** from MSWord 2000-2003— A proven indexing method.

- **Shipping Details**—Box count, weight and size.

We Design Using a Template

For authors who would like simple design at an affordable price, we offer Template Design. We can use a template design for either the cover or the text, or both. Customize a template design with your own unique photographs or art.

Template books are available in 5¼x8¼, 5½x8½ and 6x9 sizes.

Template Design Prices	
Template Cover	$135.00
Template Text	$100 for first 64 pages, $.90 per page after

Special Considerations

Template text is not for complex books with footnotes, charts, extensive photos, subchapters, or extensive front or back matter, etc.

A Template Cover includes:

- **Front cover photo:** You can give us a photo of your own to scan and place on the cover, or let us find a beautiful stock photo image for you.

- **back cover text**

- **author photo** on the back

- **background colors:** your choice from the colors below:

light background has dark title

dark background has light title

Template Text

The text layout is based on traditional book design principles that emphasize readability. We have three options: *Space Saver, Optimum* and *Large Type* (see page 39). They are all set in the same typeface, Arno Pro, with the same margins and layout. The difference between the options is the type size and leading size.

MSWord Tip

Using Styles and Formatting in MSWord to setup your book will make the text importing procedure quick and accurate (check MSWord help for details about using styles).

On our website

We Design It Section—Visit the Template Books section to learn more about template books.

Information—Visit this section to get specific Template book information and instructions such as:

- **Template Covers and Text**—Shows the text sizes and cover color and pattern choices.

- **Template Guidelines**—Use this booklet to submit your template book materials to us.

Template text design sample

If You Design it, Ready to Print

If you design your book, it must be "ready to print" in a trouble-free PDF, which means that your prepared text and cover files are printed as is. You can save money if you go this route, but designing your book to industry standards takes a lot of time and effort, as well as software knowledge and technical design details.

We can take CDs, DVDs, flash drive or 3½–inch diskettes

You design the text

When your text pages are designed, edited and finalized, you need to create a trouble-free PDF for us. We do not accept native software files. Find Ready to Print instructions on our website to help you create a PDF and send (ftp) the files direct to us.

Details to know if you are designing the cover:

- registration and crop marks
- spine width and bleeds
- document/page dimensions
- color management
- image formats and linking
- PDF creation
- 300 dpi resolution for photos
- vector vs. raster graphics

Specialized design software like Adobe InDesign, Adobe Illustrator and Quark are typically used to layout a book cover. If you do not feel comfortable in your design and software knowledge to handle this task, we would be happy to design your cover *(see page 10)*.

What we do with your files

- After you send us a trouble-free PDF of your text and/or cover, we will print a proof from your file, as is, and mail it to you.

- If you wish to correct something, you will need to change your file and send us a new PDF. Processing a new file will cost $25.00, and additional printed proofs after the first one are $40.00 each.

On our website

Information Section— Visit this section to learn the technical details of file preparation:

- **Scanning Details**—Resolution, file formats and photo optimization recommendations.

- **Softcover Guidelines**—All the measurements and details you'll need.

- **Hardcover Setup**—How to setup hardcover mockups, dustjackets and printed & laminated covers.

- **Softcover spine widths**—The dimensions for the width of your spine depending upon page count.

Bleeds or Color Pages

If your text includes bleeds or color pages, check out "Ready to Print Guidelines" on our website for details.

Photos & Logos

Photos

When printed, a photo is made up of a pattern of dots.

- TIF format is preferable to JPG
- 300 dpi resolution is best
- Black & White printing mode: Grayscale
- Offset color printing mode: CMYK
- Digital color printing mode: CMYK *or* RGB

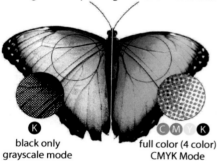

black only
grayscale mode

full color (4 color)
CMYK Mode

Logos

A logo looks best when printed in vector format rather than raster.

A vector format
like EPS or AI
is preferred.

If a vector format
is unavailable, use a
600 dpi raster image
in Bitmap mode

Getting your images

Website Images: Photo files taken from web pages are low resolution (usually 72 ppi), which is fine for screen display, but far below acceptable quality for printing.

Digital Camera: Digital cameras typically make large dimension 72 dpi JPG photo files. Using Photoshop, their dimensions can be reduced while the dpi is increased to 300. They can then be saved as tif photo files.

Scanning: Scan photos at 300 dpi and save as TIF files.

Online Stock Photos: Great looking, high quality photo files can be found at many stock photo companies online.

Photo Optimization

During optimization, the TIF photo file is resized, resolution adjusted. The darkest and lightest parts of the photo file are adjusted for best print quality.

Gorham Printing can:	Price
Optimize and place a photo file	$5.00 ea.
Scan a photo, optimize and place	$9.00 ea.

Turnaround Times

We know how anxious you are to see a finished copy of your book. Here's a breakdown of turnaround times:

Design and Proof Stage

If we design your book, you should allow 2-3 weeks for the design process depending on the complexity. We will then send you a printed proof of your entire book.

If your book is provided to us as a Ready to Print PDF, we will send you a proof typically in 3-5 business days. If there are problems outputting your file we will notify you within that same time frame.

Don't forget, additional proofs will increase the time for completion of your book.

Production Stage

The actual production of your book begins once you have given your final approval. See the production times below:

Production Stage Times		
	Digital	**Offset**
Perfect	2-3 weeks	3-4 weeks
Hardcover	6-7 weeks	7-8 weeks
Plastic spiral	3-4 weeks	4-5 weeks

What's Next?

We hope you choose us as your book printer, and we feel confident that your experience at Gorham Printing will exceed your expectations.

Get a quote:

- **online:** Use the Instant Quote or Specialized Quote.
- **or call us for a quote**

What to send us:

- **a signed quote**
- **payment:** A deposit of half down, the balance to be paid upon completion. Payment can be in the form of check or money order, VISA or Mastercard.
- **files:**
  - send from our website (FTP)
  - or, email as an attachment (5 MB max)
  - or, mail files on CD or other disk

If We Design

If we will be designing your cover or text, we will contact you with questions to begin the design process. If you have photos for us to scan and place within your text, please number your photographs to match numbers in the text file that will mark their locations.

If You Design

If you are sending Ready to Print PDF files, we will print a proof copy of the text and/or cover. Be sure to check the information section of our website for file preparation details.

After Proofing

Once you have approved the proofs, the print and binding production will begin. We will then ship them to your door, or you are welcome to pick them up if you wish.

If you are in the area, don't hesitate to stop by, discuss your project in person or take a tour of our facility.

Pricing

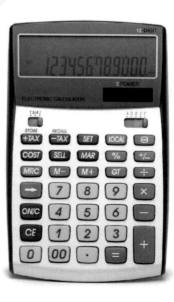

Price Lists

The Fine Print

All prices are based on manufacturing books from PDF files ready for trouble-free output. Prices do not include text design, cover design or illustration. Books with color pages result in additional charges. For other quantities of books, please contact us for quotations.

Overrun Policy

When your book is printed, an overrun may occur as we print a higher than ordered quantity to compensate for spoilage that may occur in the various printing and binding processes. Overruns are priced per book based on the quoted price minus layout and design costs.

Prices on pages 23-26 include:

- Black on 60# white paper for text pages
- Full color cover
- 10 point white C1S stock and gloss lamination* for the cover
- Perfect binding
- Digital printing for covers up to 1,300 in quantity
- Offset printing for covers above 1,300 books.

Our catalog is a sample of our standard stock and quality binding

* Matte lamination available at additional cost.

prices are per book

5¼ x 8¼			digital				offset			
PAGES	**25**	**50**	**100**	**200**	**250**	**500**	**PAGES**	**500**	**1000**	**2000**	**3000**
64	7.28	4.69	3.33	2.69	2.57	2.26	64	2.51	2.00	1.60	1.42
65-80	7.48	4.87	3.52	2.87	2.74	2.43	80	2.76	2.16	1.73	1.53
81-96	7.71	5.08	3.71	3.06	2.92	2.60	96	3.05	2.37	1.88	1.69
97-112	7.93	5.30	3.99	3.32	3.17	2.86	112	3.32	2.57	2.05	1.83
113-128	8.15	5.53	4.23	3.54	3.41	3.08	128	3.61	2.78	2.21	1.97
129-144	8.35	5.72	4.42	3.71	3.58	3.25	144	3.89	2.97	2.37	2.11
145-160	8.56	5.95	4.61	3.93	3.79	3.46	160	4.16	3.17	2.52	2.25
161-176	8.75	6.14	4.77	4.11	3.94	3.59	176	4.40	3.33	2.64	2.36
177-192	9.00	6.34	5.01	4.32	4.15	3.81	192	4.72	3.55	2.82	2.53
193-208	9.19	6.65	5.25	4.53	4.37	4.03	208	4.98	3.74	2.96	2.67
209-224	9.38	6.84	5.43	4.71	4.55	4.20	224	5.24	3.91	3.10	2.79
225-240	9.64	7.08	5.62	4.92	4.78	4.40	240	5.56	4.16	3.30	2.98
241-256	9.80	7.28	5.81	5.09	4.93	4.56	256	5.81	4.33	3.43	3.10
257-272	10.04	7.49	6.00	5.27	5.10	4.73	272	6.12	4.56	3.62	3.27
273-288	10.28	7.70	6.19	5.45	5.28	4.90	288	6.36	4.72	3.74	3.38
289-304	10.52	7.92	6.44	5.66	5.48	5.09	304	6.64	4.91	3.89	3.52
305-320	10.83	8.13	6.70	5.87	5.73	5.27	320	7.01	5.21	4.14	3.76
321-336	11.31	8.41	6.95	6.11	5.93	5.48	336	7.30	5.42	4.32	3.92
337-352	11.55	8.62	7.14	6.29	6.06	5.64	352	7.51	5.58	4.44	4.03
353-368	11.79	8.83	7.30	6.47	6.24	5.80	368	7.76	5.72	4.58	4.15
369-384	12.06	9.14	7.59	6.74	6.51	6.07	384	8.01	5.88	4.70	4.26
385-400	12.35	9.39	7.82	6.97	6.73	6.28	400	8.32	6.11	4.89	4.44
401-416	12.58	9.60	8.01	7.18	6.98	6.53	416	8.60	6.32	5.06	4.59
417-432	12.82	9.81	8.20	7.35	7.15	6.69	432	8.86	6.50	5.20	4.72
433-448	13.31	10.16	8.49	7.56	7.39	6.92	448	9.16	6.71	5.37	4.88
449-464	13.55	10.37	8.67	7.73	7.56	7.08	464	9.42	6.89	5.51	5.01
465-480	13.79	10.48	8.81	7.91	7.69	7.25	480	9.97	7.36	5.94	5.42
481-496	14.02	10.68	9.00	8.08	7.89	7.41	496	10.25	7.57	6.10	5.57

Prices Effective 1/2010, Subject to Change without Notice

prices are per book

5½ x 8½			digital					offset		
PAGES	25	50	100	200	250	500	PAGES	500	1000	2000	3000
64	8.05	5.18	3.69	2.95	2.82	2.47	64	2.51	2.00	1.60	1.42
65-80	8.32	5.45	3.93	3.20	3.06	2.71	80	2.76	2.16	1.73	1.53
81-96	8.59	5.69	4.18	3.44	3.28	2.92	96	3.05	2.37	1.88	1.69
97-112	8.88	5.96	4.50	3.74	3.58	3.22	112	3.32	2.57	2.05	1.83
113-128	9.16	6.28	4.77	4.01	3.85	3.48	128	3.61	2.78	2.21	1.97
129-144	9.44	6.54	5.02	4.26	4.10	3.72	144	3.89	2.97	2.37	2.11
145-160	9.74	6.79	5.31	4.51	4.37	3.93	160	4.16	3.17	2.52	2.25
161-176	10.01	7.02	5.56	4.75	4.56	4.15	176	4.40	3.33	2.64	2.36
177-192	10.27	7.34	5.84	5.05	4.85	4.44	192	4.72	3.55	2.82	2.53
193-208	10.54	7.70	6.11	5.32	5.14	4.72	208	4.98	3.74	2.96	2.67
209-224	10.81	7.96	6.36	5.52	5.38	4.95	224	5.24	3.91	3.10	2.79
225-240	11.15	8.23	6.65	5.84	5.66	5.27	240	5.56	4.16	3.30	2.98
241-256	11.44	8.49	6.91	6.09	5.90	5.50	256	5.81	4.33	3.43	3.10
257-272	11.76	8.77	7.17	6.33	6.14	5.73	272	6.12	4.56	3.62	3.27
273-288	12.07	9.05	7.42	6.58	6.38	5.87	288	6.36	4.72	3.74	3.38
289-304	12.39	9.33	7.68	6.78	6.64	6.11	304	6.64	4.91	3.89	3.52
305-320	12.74	9.74	8.02	7.15	6.91	6.47	320	7.01	5.21	4.14	3.76
321-336	13.00	10.02	8.33	7.44	7.17	6.75	336	7.30	5.42	4.31	3.92
337-352	13.31	10.30	8.58	7.69	7.41	6.98	352	7.51	5.58	4.44	4.03
353-368	13.62	10.52	8.84	7.93	7.65	7.20	368	7.76	5.72	4.58	4.15
369-384	13.93	10.79	9.10	8.17	7.88	7.43	384	8.01	5.88	4.70	4.26
385-400	14.29	11.12	9.40	8.34	8.17	7.65	400	8.32	6.11	4.89	4.44
401-416	14.81	11.44	9.65	8.61	8.47	7.93	416	8.60	6.32	5.06	4.59
417-432	15.12	11.72	9.91	8.84	8.70	8.15	432	8.86	6.50	5.20	4.72
433-448	15.68	12.14	10.19	9.16	9.01	8.44	448	9.16	6.71	5.37	4.88
449-464	15.99	12.42	10.44	9.39	9.24	8.67	464	9.42	6.89	5.51	5.01
465-480	16.47	12.93	11.01	9.94	9.79	9.20	480	9.97	7.36	5.94	5.42
481-496	16.78	13.20	11.26	10.18	10.03	9.43	496	10.25	7.57	6.10	5.57

Prices Effective 1/2010, Subject to Change without Notice

prices are per book

6 x 9				digital			offset			
PAGES	25	50	100	200	250	500	PAGES	500	1000	2000	3000
64	8.05	5.18	3.69	2.95	2.82	2.47	64	2.57	2.05	1.65	1.46
65-80	8.32	5.45	3.93	3.20	3.06	2.71	80	2.83	2.22	1.78	1.58
81-96	8.59	5.69	4.18	3.44	3.28	2.92	96	3.13	2.44	1.95	1.75
97-112	8.88	5.96	4.50	3.74	3.58	3.22	112	3.42	2.66	2.12	1.90
113-128	9.16	6.28	4.77	4.01	3.85	3.48	128	3.72	2.88	2.30	2.05
129-144	9.44	6.54	5.02	4.26	4.10	3.72	144	4.01	3.08	2.46	2.20
145-160	9.74	6.79	5.31	4.51	4.37	3.93	160	4.29	3.29	2.62	2.35
161-176	10.01	7.02	5.56	4.75	4.56	4.15	176	4.55	3.46	2.76	2.46
177-192	10.27	7.34	5.84	5.05	4.85	4.44	192	4.88	3.68	2.94	2.65
193-208	10.54	7.70	6.11	5.32	5.14	4.72	208	5.16	3.89	3.10	2.80
209-224	10.81	7.96	6.36	5.52	5.38	4.95	224	5.44	4.08	3.24	2.93
225-240	11.15	8.23	6.65	5.84	5.66	5.27	240	5.78	4.33	3.45	3.13
241-256	11.44	8.49	6.91	6.09	5.90	5.50	256	6.04	4.52	3.60	3.26
257-272	11.76	8.77	7.17	6.33	6.14	5.73	272	6.36	4.75	3.79	3.44
273-288	12.07	9.05	7.42	6.58	6.38	5.87	288	6.62	4.93	3.92	3.56
289-304	12.39	9.33	7.68	6.78	6.64	6.11	304	6.90	5.13	4.08	3.70
305-320	12.74	9.74	8.02	7.15	6.91	6.47	320	7.29	5.43	4.34	3.95
321-336	13.00	10.02	8.33	7.44	7.17	6.75	336	7.60	5.66	4.52	4.12
337-352	13.31	10.30	8.58	7.69	7.41	6.98	352	7.81	5.83	4.65	4.24
353-368	13.62	10.52	8.84	7.93	7.65	7.20	368	8.08	5.98	4.81	4.37
369-384	13.93	10.79	9.10	8.17	7.88	7.43	384	8.33	6.15	4.94	4.49
385-400	14.29	11.12	9.40	8.34	8.17	7.65	400	8.66	6.39	5.14	4.68
401-416	14.81	11.44	9.65	8.61	8.47	7.93	416	8.94	6.60	5.31	4.83
417-432	15.12	11.72	9.91	8.84	8.70	8.15	432	9.22	6.79	5.46	4.97
433-448	15.68	12.14	10.19	9.16	9.01	8.44	448	9.53	7.02	5.64	5.14
449-464	15.99	12.42	10.44	9.39	9.24	8.67	464	9.80	7.21	5.79	5.28
465-480	16.47	12.93	11.01	9.94	9.79	9.20	480	10.37	7.69	6.24	5.71
481-496	16.78	13.20	11.26	10.18	10.03	9.43	496	10.67	7.90	6.41	5.86

Prices Effective 1/2010, Subject to Change without Notice

prices are per book

8¼ x 10¾				digital			8½x11		offset		
PAGES	25	50	100	200	250	500	PAGES	500	1000	2000	3000
64	8.12	5.53	4.24	3.54	3.41	3.08	64	3.51	2.72	2.28	2.14
65-80	8.48	5.91	4.58	3.90	3.75	3.42	80	4.00	3.04	2.52	2.37
81-96	8.89	6.27	4.94	4.26	4.08	3.74	96	4.49	3.38	2.78	2.61
97-112	9.31	6.78	5.44	4.71	4.56	4.20	112	5.03	3.76	3.08	2.88
113-128	9.72	7.22	5.82	5.10	4.95	4.57	128	5.55	4.12	3.37	3.14
129-144	10.10	7.60	6.18	5.45	5.29	4.91	144	6.07	4.49	3.66	3.40
145-160	10.52	7.95	6.58	5.81	5.68	5.22	160	6.54	4.81	3.93	3.65
161-176	10.91	8.27	6.94	6.15	5.94	5.53	176	7.01	5.13	4.18	3.87
177-192	11.28	8.70	7.32	6.56	6.34	5.92	192	7.55	5.52	4.49	4.16
193-208	11.86	9.17	7.72	6.95	6.76	6.34	208	8.08	5.89	4.79	4.43
209-224	12.23	9.54	8.07	7.24	7.09	6.66	224	8.55	6.21	5.03	4.66
225-240	12.67	9.86	8.44	7.64	7.44	7.05	240	9.11	6.61	5.36	4.96
241-256	13.07	10.23	8.79	7.98	7.78	7.37	256	9.60	6.95	5.63	5.20
257-272	13.49	10.62	9.15	8.32	8.12	7.70	272	10.08	7.29	5.88	5.43
273-288	13.92	11.00	9.51	8.67	8.46	7.92	288	10.56	7.61	6.13	5.65
289-304	14.35	11.49	9.92	8.98	8.84	8.28	304	10.99	7.95	6.39	5.89
305-320	14.72	11.94	10.29	9.39	9.12	8.67	320	11.61	8.42	6.79	6.26
321-336	15.24	12.43	10.75	9.83	9.52	9.09	336	12.14	8.80	7.10	6.54
337-352	15.66	12.81	11.10	10.17	9.85	9.42	352	12.61	9.12	7.34	6.76
353-368	16.08	13.13	11.46	10.51	10.18	9.74	368	13.09	9.45	7.60	6.99
369-384	16.60	13.62	11.93	10.96	10.62	10.17	384	13.60	9.82	7.88	7.25
385-400	17.07	14.05	12.34	11.19	11.00	10.46	400	14.15	10.22	8.21	7.55
401-416	17.69	14.51	12.77	11.68	11.55	10.99	416	14.78	10.69	8.61	7.93
417-432	18.11	14.89	13.13	12.01	11.89	11.31	432	15.28	11.04	8.88	8.18
433-448	18.77	15.41	13.49	12.42	12.29	11.69	448	15.84	11.45	9.21	8.48
449-464	19.19	15.79	13.84	12.75	12.62	12.01	464	16.34	11.80	9.49	8.73
465-480	19.41	16.07	14.19	13.09	12.95	12.33	480	17.17	12.48	10.09	9.31
481-496	19.83	16.45	14.54	13.42	13.28	12.65	496	17.67	12.83	10.37	9.56

Prices Effective 1/2010, Subject to Change without Notice

Printing Methods

Depending upon the number of books you would like to print, we use two different production methods: digital and offset. Both have their unique advantages:

Digital
for 25-500 books

Advantages

- Cost effective for short runs.

- Faster turnaround time.

- Less expensive to make changes for reprints.

- Color interior pages available.

Offset
for 500-3,000 books

Advantages

- Higher quality photos and screens.

- Colored and textured papers available. Coated paper is also available for hardcover books.

- Using a larger sheet size enables more options for hardcover binding.

Full Color Text Pages

In the past, short run, full color books printed offset have been expensive. However, recent advancements in digital color printer technology make digital full color printing of between 25 and 500 books an affordable option.

Full color printing does cost more than single color (black only) printing. To reduce the cost, consider grouping your color images together as much as possible. We print full color text pages only digitally, not offset.

Comparison of 64 page, 6x9 book					
Quantities	**100**	**200**	**300**	**400**	**500**
64 pages: all B & W	$3.69	$2.95	$2.71	$2.56	$2.47
64 pages: 32 color, 32 B & W, grouped	$6.32	$5.31	$4.82	$4.58	$4.41
64 pages: 32 color, 32 B & W, interspersed	$6.83	$5.88	$5.38	$5.13	$4.94
64 pages: all color	$7.36	$6.32	$5.85	$5.62	$5.44

Pros and Cons of Digital Color

One advantage of digital color printing is that setup is greatly reduced, as no negatives or plates are used. Also, color file types are more flexible, using either a CMYK or RGB workflow interchangeably.

One difficulty in digital color printing is matching color. All color printers are different. We cannot match exactly to your color printout, although we will strive to come as close as possible.

prices are per book

5¼ x 8¼	digital full color					
		50	100	200	300	400	500
PAGES	100	8.64	6.94	5.99	5.55	5.32	5.14
	200	12.77	10.72	9.36	8.76	8.47	8.36
	300	17.07	14.59	12.62	12.08	11.92	11.83

Prices Effective 1/2010, Subject to Change without Notice

prices are per book

5½ x 8½ or 6 x 9	digital full color					
		50	100	200	300	400	500
PAGES	100	11.84	9.90	8.61	8.02	7.73	7.62
	200	18.95	16.12	14.43	14.11	13.97	13.88
	300	25.94	21.95	20.64	20.32	20.16	20.06

Prices Effective 1/2010, Subject to Change without Notice

prices are per book

8¼ x 10¾	digital full color					
		50	100	200	300	400	500
PAGES	100	12.01	10.32	9.12	8.58	8.30	8.20
	200	19.50	16.98	15.35	15.07	14.95	14.84
	300	26.92	23.15	21.86	21.58	21.44	21.36

Prices Effective 1/2010, Subject to Change without Notice

Bindings

Perfect Binding (softcover)

Often called a "trade paperback", this binding uses hot flexible glue, and must have a minimum of 64 pages and maximum of 512. As an example, this catalog is perfect bound.

Casebinding (hardcover)

The most durable binding method. The page signatures are sewn together, (smyth sewn if offset, oversewn if digital) reinforced and attached to the hardcover, typically covered with bookcloth, imitation leather or a printed and laminated paper.

Plastic Spiral Binding

An ideal binding for books that must open and lie flat, such as cookbooks, work-books, teachers' guides or manuals.

Optional Extras

At additional cost, you can dress up your book with foiling and embossing

An option for hardcover books, is a printed and laminated cover, where printed paper is used for the binding material.

We can also print a dustjacket to wrap over your hardcover book.

Binding Price Comparison

Many have asked, "how much more is a hardcover book compared to a softcover book?" Below is a cost comparison of the binding styles we offer.

prices are per book

Specifications

- 6 x 9 trim size
- 192 pages
- ready to print cover and text files
- black text on white 60# Weyerhaeuser Husky Offset

Binding Style	500 books	1000 books
Perfect Bound book with 4 color, laminated, 10 pt. cover	4.88	3.68
Plastic Spiral Bound book with 4 color, laminated, 10 pt. cover	5.92	4.68
Hardcover book smyth sewn, Arrestox book cloth, foil stamping on front and spine	10.35	8.23
Hardcover book with dustjacket smyth sewn, Arrestox book cloth, foil stamping on front and spine, with 4 color, laminated, 100 lb. dustjacket	12.44	9.78
Printed and Laminated Hardcover book smyth sewn with printed and laminated 4 color cover	11.25	8.81

Prices Effective 1/2010, Subject to Change without Notice

Landscape formats (books bound on the short side) usually incur added expense. Inquire for a specialized quotation.

The ROBIN FAMILY

Grant and Frances Valentine

Packaging and Shipping

After your book has been completed, it is packed for shipping. We use 8½ x 11 x 12 inch or 9 x 12 x 12 inch boxes, depending on the book size. Our carrier of choice is United Parcel Service.

See the chart at right to determine the approximate weight of each box, depending upon the number of pages and book dimensions. Typically, the boxes for 6 x 9 books weigh 43 lbs. each and the 5½ x 8½ and 8½ x 11 boxes weigh 34 lbs. each.

Approximate weight and count per carton

PAGES	5¼ x 8¼ or 5½ x 8½	6 x 9	8¼ x 10¾ or 8½ x 11
64	142	150	71
96	100	102	50
128	78	78	39
160	62	66	31
192	54	56	27
240	42	46	21
288	36	38	18
320	32	34	16
352	30	32	15
384	26	28	13
weight	34 lbs.	43 lbs.	34 lbs.

Page Structure

Typesetting

Choosing a Typeface

Traditionally, typefaces for books have *serifs* on their letterforms. Serifs are the strokes that project from the top or bottom of the main stroke of the letter. They assist readability by keeping the reader's eye flowing horizontally across the words. Although typefaces without serifs *(sans serif)* are increasingly popular, they are not comfortable for reading an extended amount of type as in books.

The tone or feeling of the typeface is of utmost importance. Although somewhat subjectively, most typefaces exude an impression, which, if used with complementary subject matter can enhance the mood of the writing.

"First and foremost, the forms of the letters themselves contribute much to legibility or its opposite."

—Jan Tschichold, *The Form of the Book*

Traditional Rules
of Typography for Books

Book design (or typesetting) does not follow the same rules that are taught in a most keyboarding classes. When setting up text pages, the following guidelines will help you in producing professional-looking pages.

1. Book text is usually *justified,* spanning the width of the text column between the margins.

2. Italics should be used for emphasis. Avoid using all caps, underlining or bold type.

3. Books are often set somewhat smaller than 12 points. Check copies of books you enjoy reading and you will probably be surprised at the size of the type.

4. Use only one space after periods for ease in justification.

5. Use indents at the beginning of each paragraph rather than gaps or open areas between paragraphs. Indents should be small (.25 of an inch). An exception is the first paragraph of a chapter or new section, which should not be indented.

6. Leading is a specific numeric measurement, and is not the same as "double-spacing" in word-processing software. Default leading is generally 25% more than the point size of the type.

Definitions:

Point Size

The unit of measure for the size of letters. There are 12 points in one pica and 6 picas in one inch.

Leading (rhymes with sledding)

The space between lines of type.

Our Favorite Typefaces

The typeface chosen for the body text (the main story of the book) is particularly important to the book's overall mood. For example, an instructive manual on engineering might be best set in a blocky, vertical face with an angular feeling; but a romance novel might have a flowery, round typeface with an attractive set of italics. The reader will probably never really look directly at each letter of the typeface—its mood will be subtly conveyed.

Arno Pro

ABCDEFGHIJKLMNOPQRSTUVWXYZ
abcdefghijklmnopqrstuvwxyz1234567890 ½&;!?"

Arno is a new design by Robert Slimbach, inspired by the Italian Renaissance. It is warm and readable—a modern take on a traditional style. The font family includes an array of swashes, weights and characters, making it a very well-rounded typeface for books.

Bembo

ABCDEFGHIJKLMNOPQRSTUVWXYZ
abcdefghijklmnopqrstuvwxyz1234567890 ½&;!?"

Bembo is arguably the most readable typeface of all and works in any type of book. Derived from the Aldus typeface of the Renaissance, it is proportioned well and is quiet and simple.

Garamond

ABCDEFGHIJKLMNOPQRSTUVWXYZ
abcdefghijklmnopqrstuvwxyz1234567890 ½&;!?"

Garamond was designed in the 1500s, but it has a timeless appeal. The letterforms are open and round, resulting in a highly readable typeface. It has a soft feeling, and is well-suited to poetry books and novels.

Minion

ABCDEFGHIJKLMNOPQRSTUVWXYZ
abcdefghijklmnopqrstuvwxyz 1234567890 ½&;!?"

Minion is a very modern typeface, designed by Robert Slimbach in 1990 and inspired by classical Renaissance typefaces. It is very readable and applicable for any style of book. We use Minion more than any other typeface. It is the primary typeface used in this catalog.

Warnock

ABCDEFGHIJKLMNOPQRSTUVWXYZ
abcdefghijklmnopqrstuvwxyz1234567890 ½&;!?"

Designed just a decade ago, Warnock is a fully modern typeface—with classical sensibilities—designed with modern digital printing and onscreen viewing in mind. Its sharp clean look reads and prints well.

Margins and Words per Page

¾ INCH

Sularbit. Nocurbit. Cit, cuppl. Fice ac ta, nocchuius, quit, escesente aris Mulina, Cupimulos re nordientem simihil icondactus atienat quam publis terma, que et iptere consula consum cenatin tescris. Omnovem, utem acivit; nonsta dum quam erit. Si consilis inatu conculis, mentes intribensus, si cidiem noc terfecendam termihil vigna imo conste, quodi, consul commovere, vagin ium concultuam publiaet ius ia L. Fulius; hui et dum supimil iumus; noculla ribuntid renterid ca pre res, non tuit.

Nitemno nequam nonsulla ituitantique factorum at, que deatia me consi consum inprem mentifex num orae, vit, consunt ernius hocre cre poponstre tus latiam iam incum res serio ca; nicente morionsimus acta, nit; et ne et? Aximil conoctus, Palici ingultortus, cae temquos, onnnimno vitret L. Nihi, quam te, P. Equam pos hoccior untemus, cres rem catquo ia int.

Vivilicae aucii publint, nor hortuit vitu it ves consus, potil con dicidet, es obunter riptea con Etra, quos et inpributu iae aut L. Ifferfecrit fac vaginatum poentidea nocultur ina, quidium evoctam omnihin sendessilis ponfenat oca; Catur, qua ver hebemur. Suncur acit? Muliisq ultimpestro egerium verfica vide converf icidet abentuam dicatus ius M. Batu quita Satod C. Otandac ipientessis. Ad sus virmandam, nihilicae nihilicatu me cus, quam re iam morid delari et? quam publi pravoltuam prius es amdiis inte facibus facta vid fue publi, quam nem se tu conscere tanum iam Romanti publi incem aucessideti, ella re, crum medio, quis, fuide tusula centre cenius? Hem orae no. Mulibunclus condius, patus, ubilius satius abessim abessim sentemum inti, quam fatorum publiac emoente ilaressente, fore enihil habes con tasto C. Seror horae, vit iae med consuam et L. Serdi, conveniquit; ipiontiam. Ena, patu vium tin pes audentervis ortant.

Faucon itabi se, consimunum publist? Ahae tem. Us verfenatumPateremo ratatu it faccips, que a nons videface perum autus peris apescip senatumunus

¾ INCH

¾ INCH

1 INCH

Smaller format margins

General margins for 5¼ x 8¼, 5½ x 8½ and 6 x 9 books are a minimum of ¾ of an inch.

Larger format margins

For larger format books, it is best to give the type lots of "air" all around for readability. The maximum line width on a 8¼ x 10¾ or 8½ x 11 book should be five-inches for a single column. Photos can utilize the space outside of the text. You can opt for two narrower columns instead, but this can make a more complex design.

1½ INCHES

Sularbit. Nocurbit. Cit, cuppl. Fice ac ta, nocchuius, quit, escesente aris Mulina, Cupimulos re nordientem simihil icondactus atienat quam publis terma, que et iptere consula consum cenatin tescris. Omnovem, utem acivit; nonsta dum quam erit. Si consilis inatu conculis, mentes intribensus, si cidiem noc terfecendam termihil vigna imo conste, quodi, consul commovere, vagin ium concultuam publiaet ius ia L. Fulius; hui et dum supimil iumus; noculla ribuntid renterid ca pre res, non tuit.

Nitemno nequam nonsulla ituitantique factorum at, que deatia me consi consum inprem mentifex num orae, vit, consunt ernius hocre cre poponstre tus latiam iam incum res serio ca; nicente morionsimus acta, nit; et ne et? Aximil conoctus, Palici ingultortus, onnnimno vitret L. Nihi, quam te, P. Equam pos hoccior untemus, cres rem catquo ia int.

Vivilicae aucii publint, nor hortuit vitu it ves consus, potil con dicidet, es obunter riptea con Etra, quos et inpributu iae aut L. Ifferfecrit fac vaginatum poentidea nocultur ina, quidium avoctam omnihin sendessilis ponfenat oca; Catur, qua ver hebemur. Suncur acit? Muliisq ultimpestro egerium verfica vide converf icidet abentuam dicatus ius M. Batu quita Satod C. Otandac ipientessis. Ad sus virmandam, nihilicae nihilicatu me cus, quam re iam morid delari et? quam publi pravoltuam prius es amdiis inte facibus facta vid fue publi, quam nem se tu conscere tanum iam cem aucessideti, ella re, crum medio, quis, fuide tusula centre cenius? Hem orae no. Mulibunclus condius, patus, ubilius satius abessim sentemum inti, quam fatorum publiac emoente ilaressente, fore enihil habes con tasto C. Seror horae, vit iae med consuam et L. Serdi, conveniquit; ipiontiam. Ena, patu vium tin pes audentervis ortant.

Faccips, que a nons videface perum autus peris apescip senatumunus-Mulem avo, Catiam dicaedi, se nerfectus vervidem temorum terum mo inam tampro es loculest vignati ampervilic mententris An vagina, consim perfec vitium occivid Catqua publibuntera mena L. It.

Ectus hocam deps, num pra des, publint eatquo mors sente culeriam pero iam quon Et Vivehemenare inatur quam et, qua praectus vivita quam quonsula re co Catil vitra consuli ctorit.

1¾ INCHES

1¾ INCHES

2 INCHES

How many words on a page?

Arno Pro: 10.7 point type / 15 point leading SPACE SAVER

The typeface chosen for a book is perhaps the most important aspect of the whole design. Each typeface will convey a particular mood to the writing, subconsciously supporting the feelings evoked by the words. In this computer age of thousands of typefaces produced by many manufacturers, with trendy new faces designed every day, those that reign have proven themselves over years of typesetting use.

approximate words per page:
5½ x 8½: 400   6 x 9: 425

Arno Pro: 11.7 point type / 16 point leading OPTIMUM

The typeface chosen for a book is perhaps the most important aspect of the whole design. Each typeface will convey a particular mood to the writing, subconsciously supporting the feelings evoked by the words. In this computer age of thousands of typefaces produced by many manufacturers, with trendy new faces designed every day, those that reign have proven themselves over years of typesetting use.

approximate words per page:
5½ x 8½: 350   6 x 9: 400

Arno Pro: 12.2 point type / 16.5 point leading LARGE TYPE

The typeface chosen for a book is perhaps the most important aspect of the whole design. Each typeface will convey a particular mood to the writing, subconsciously supporting the feelings evoked by the words. In this computer age of thousands of typefaces produced by many manufacturers, with trendy new faces designed every day, those that reign have proven themselves over years of typesetting use.

approximate words per page:
5½ x 8½: 300   6x9: 350

Headers and Numbers

Headers at the top of each page or footers at the bottom of each page are a design option. They are not necessary in every case; for novels and poetry books a simple page number is sufficient. Traditionally, the author's name appears on the left and the book's title on the right. In reference books, cookbooks and manuals, the chapter name is sometimes used in the header.

It is best to set headers as small caps with wide letterspacing in a heavy version of the body text typeface. Headers should be set at 8 or 9 points, depending upon the typeface. Headers are usually best aligned to the outside top margin of every page, with the page number on the extreme outside (there should be at least .2 inches between the number and the header).

Page Number Placement

Page numbers can be placed at the top outsides, bottom outsides or bottom centers. However, they should not be placed all on the left or all on the right. If placed in this manner, the page numbers will not line up back to back.

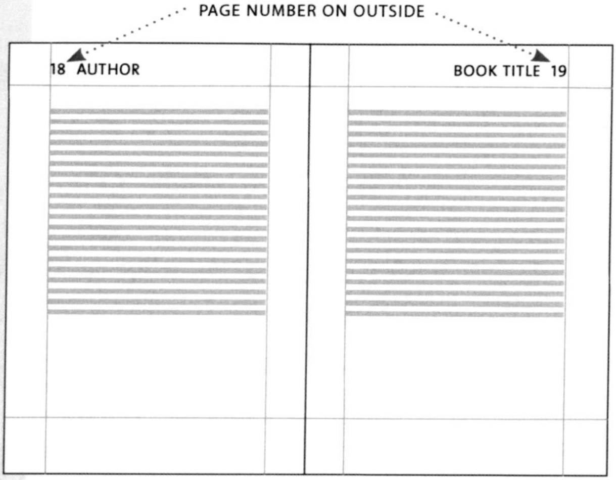

PAGE NUMBER ON OUTSIDE

18 AUTHOR

BOOK TITLE 19

Footnotes

Footnotes should appear at the bottom of the page with their corresponding number and should be within the text block boundary. They are usually set two point sizes smaller than the body text; 8 point type on 9 point leading is a good rule of thumb. There should be about .25 of an inch of space between the top of the footnote and the body text.

The footnote should always be set flush left and justified only when extremely long (6 lines or more).

Footnotes are often set with a .5 point line rule over them to distinguish them from the body text. The line should always span the column. If no line is used, the text of the footnote can be italicized to distinguish it from the body text. This should be avoided if possible because often there are italicized references in the footnote that would then have to be *un*-italicized to set *them* apart.

The number of the footnote should be super-scripted, but care should be taken that it does not get too small for readability.[1]

---

[1] This is an example of a good way to set the type of a footnote.

Chapter Headlines

The first page of every chapter usually contains a chapter number and headline at the top and a page number at the bottom. There are numerous design approaches one can take for these pages, which often depend upon the book's subject matter. For example, a headline for a book with a serious subject matter would be better set with everything flush left, while fiction and personal-history books look more "friendly" with chapter numbers and headlines centered. Some suggested designs we offer are as follows:

STYLE 1—All flush left

STYLE 2—All centered

CHAPTER ONE
Headline

The typeface chosen for a book is perhaps the most important aspect of the whole design. Each typeface will convey a particular mood to the writing, unconsciously supporting the feelings invoked by the words. In this computer age of thousands of typefaces produced by many manufacturers, with trendy new faces designed every day, those that reign have proven themselves over years of typesetting use.

Readability is paramount—the spaces between letters, words and lines of type all assist or inhibit comfortable legibility. As Jan Tschichold so wisely stated: "Perfect typography depends on perfect harmony between all of its elements." This harmony is achieved by careful observation of the parts *and* the whole. A book that is improperly set can annoy the reader, in turn destroying the author's intended message, but a well-designed page will invite your eyes to read without distraction.

The typeface chosen for a book is perhaps the most important aspect of the whole design. Each typeface will convey a particular mood to the writing, unconsciously supporting the feelings invoked by the words. In this computer age of thousands of typefaces produced by many manufacturers, with trendy new faces designed every day, those that reign have proven themselves over years of typesetting use.

Readability is paramount—the spaces between letters, words and lines of type all assist or inhibit comfortable legibility. As Jan Tschichold so wisely

13

STYLE 3—All flush right

CHAPTER ONE
Headline

The typeface chosen for a book is perhaps the most important aspect of the whole design. Each typeface will convey a particular mood to the writing, unconsciously supporting the feelings invoked by the words. In this computer age of thousands of typefaces produced by many manufacturers, with trendy new faces designed every day, those that reign have proven themselves over years of typesetting use.

Readability is paramount—the spaces between letters, words and lines of type all assist or inhibit comfortable legibility. As Jan Tschichold so wisely stated: "Perfect typography depends on perfect harmony between all of its elements." This harmony is achieved by careful observation of the parts *and* the whole. A book that is improperly set can annoy the reader, in turn destroying the author's intended message, but a well-designed page will invite your eyes to read without distraction.

The typeface chosen for a book is perhaps the most important aspect of the whole design. Each typeface will convey a particular mood to the writing, unconsciously supporting the feelings invoked by the words. In this computer age of thousands of typefaces produced by many manufacturers, with trendy new faces designed every day, those that reign have proven themselves over years of typesetting use.

Readability is paramount—the spaces between letters, words and lines of type all assist or inhibit comfortable legibility. As Jan Tschichold so wisely stated: "Perfect typography depends on

13

STYLE 4—for 8½ x 11″ books, two columns

The Front Matter

Following are the guidelines we use when formatting the front matter pages. Each book is different, and not all of these pages are necessary in every book, but this order is the industry standard.

The headlines of these pages are usually about 4-8 points bigger than the text point size and should be designed differently than the chapter headlines. To further set them apart from the chapter headlines, they should start lower on the page, have wider or lesser space between the headline and text, or be set with a different left-to-right alignment.

Front matter page numbering

Front matter is often not included in the page numbering of a book. Often Page 1 will start on the first page of Chapter One. If there are many pages of front matter, they are often numbered separately using lowercase Roman numerals.

Right or Left?

Traditionally, chapters were started on right-hand (recto) pages only. Current industry standards use the next-available page. The standards and conventions of setting up what belongs on a right hand or left hand page are only that—standards and conventions. There are many instances in which these standards may not be applicable or desirable.

Title Page

The Title page is the one page that creates a transition between the cover and the text pages. Since a decorative face is usually chosen for the book's cover, the title is often set in a smaller version of the cover type. The author's name can be set in the same face used on the cover, or the same typeface as the text face.

This page is always on the right-hand side. It may include a small piece of artwork relating to the cover, or a small graphical element between the title and author. A page number never appears on this page.

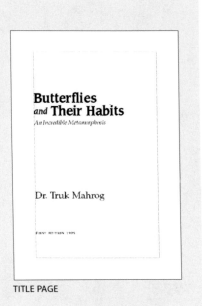

TITLE PAGE

Front Matter Order

1. Title Page
2. Copyright
3. Dedication
4. Foreword
5. Contents
6. Preface
7. Acknowledgments
8. Introduction

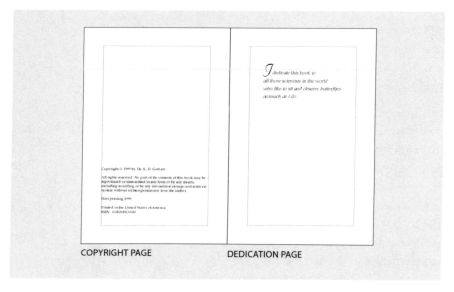

COPYRIGHT PAGE

DEDICATION PAGE

Copyright Page

This page is always on the left. The type size is smaller than that used for the body of the text, but it is usually the same face. It can be set flush left, centered or flush right, depending upon how the rest of the book is set up. It is usually set up so the last line falls at the bottom margin boundary. A page number never appears on this page.

Dedication Page

The Dedication is usually across from the Copyright page. Often it is set in italics or with a decorative first letter of script or italics (a simulation of handwriting, an implication to the reader that this is a personal note from the author). It is usually set a few points bigger than the point size of the body text. Again, it should follow the format of the rest of the book and be aligned either centered, flush-right or flush-left. It is usually set either in the middle of the page, or approximately three inches from

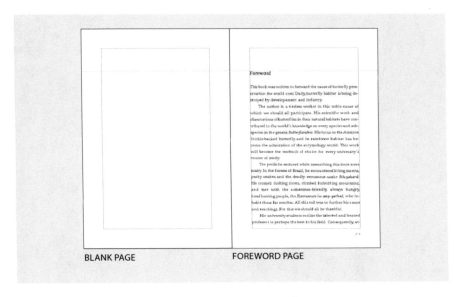

BLANK PAGE   FOREWORD PAGE

Foreword

the top page boundary to distinguish it from the tops of the text pages. It is often unnecessary to have the word "Dedication" on top, because the text usually is worded in such a way for that to be redundant (i.e.: *I dedicate this book to my mother…*).

A Foreword is generally written about the book by someone other than the author and is usually about 2-4 pages long. If there is a Foreword, it should appear on the next available right-hand page after the Dedication, and the left-hand page should be blank. Note the spelling of "Foreword"—think of "before the words."

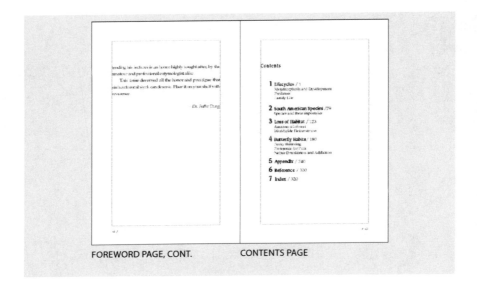

FOREWORD PAGE, CONT.   CONTENTS PAGE

Contents

The words "Table of Contents" have gone out of favor in recent years; "Contents" is deemed sufficient. Almost all books contain a Contents page, however, some do not. If you decide to have a Contents page, all sections and chapters should be included, plus subheadlines if it is a technical work. It should start at the top of the page in the same location as the rest of the front matter with a similarly designed headline. When chapter names are short, *leaders* (a line of dots) can be used between the chapter and its corresponding page number. If the chapter names are long, page numbers can be placed closer and without leaders.

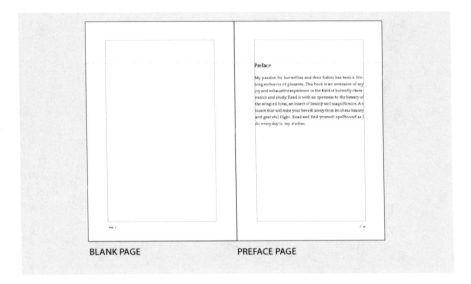

BLANK PAGE   PREFACE PAGE

Preface

The Preface is written by the author and contains the reasons for writing the book and the research undertaken. If there is a Preface, it should appear on the next available right-hand page after the Contents, and the left-hand page should be blank or include the end of the Contents.

How Low?

The front matter pages usually start lower down on the page than the first pages of the chapters. The Dedication, Foreword, Contents, Preface, Acknowledgments and Introduction all start consistently at the same location on the page. The two exceptions are: the title page which is placed on the page wherever it looks most balanced and the copyright page, where the text is placed to line up at the bottom.

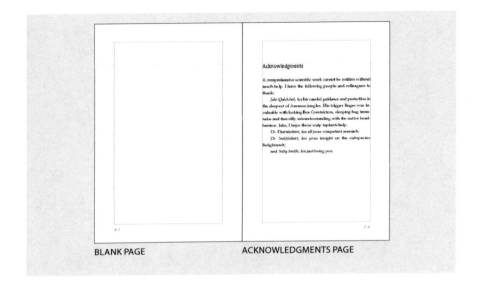

BLANK PAGE   ACKNOWLEDGMENTS PAGE

Acknowledgments

The Acknowledgments page is the author's area to thank all those people who assisted in any phases of the book's production. It should appear on the next available right-hand page after the Preface, and the left-hand page should be blank or include the end of the Preface.

Introduction

The introduction contains material relevant to the text and should be read before the rest of the book, for example, the historical background for the book. It should appear just before the first chapter, and should start on a right-hand page.

The Back Matter

The back matter type size is sometimes smaller than the rest of the body text since it is used for reference. The headlines for back matter should be set in the same manner as the front matter and start in the same location on the page. Not all books require all of these pages, but this order is the industry standard.

Appendix

The appendix usually contains explanations that help clarify the text, such as laws, documents, lists, charts and tables.

Endnotes

When a notation or explanation is too large for a footnote, it should appear as an endnote at the back.

Glossary

An alphabetical glossary is useful in a technical work with complicated terms that require explanation.

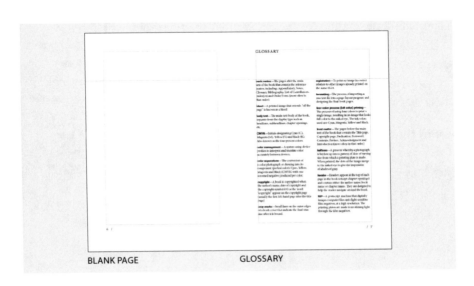

BLANK PAGE   GLOSSARY

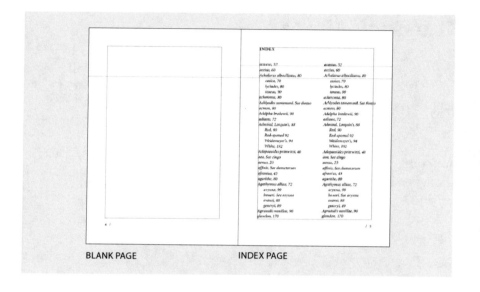

BLANK PAGE   INDEX PAGE

Bibliography

There are many ways to set up a bibliography, depending on the style of the book or how many sources were used. Check the *Chicago Manual of Style* for specific information.

About the author

If you do not have this on the back cover, you can place it within the back matter.

Index

On our website, we offer instructions on how to tag your files so we can automatically create an index when we format your book, using MSWord's indexing capabilities.

Order Form

This page is usually set on the book's last right-hand page with a blank back-side so the reader can cut or tear it out if necessary. It should be clear and concise.

Entering the Marketplace

Copyright

To copyright your book, place a notice on the copyright page. Either the word *copyright* and/or the © symbol must appear along with the year of first publication and the name of the copyright owner (see example).

Copyright © 2009
Bill Shakespeare
All rights reserved.

You may then elaborate on the *all rights reserved* phrase if you wish. Check other books for accepted variations.

Registering your copyright

After your book is printed, you may register your copyright by sending the following items to the U.S. Copyright Office: Form CO, a $50 fee and two copies of your book (one if it is not for sale).

Registering your work officially recognizes you as the copyright holder. Although recommended, it is not absolutely necessary to register your work. Copyright is secured automatically when the work is created. Registration strengthens your legal position. More information on this subject is available at www.copyright.gov.

Contact

Information Phone
(202) 707-3000

Forms Request Phone
(202) 707-9100

Online
www.copyright.gov

Library of Congress Control Number

Getting your book into libraries

These numbers are issued prior to publication, and are reserved for books intended for distribution to libraries. The number is called the Preassigned Control Number (PCN) and may be requested by submitting a one-page application to the Library of Congress. The number is then printed on the copyright page of your book, preceded by the phrase, *Library of Congress Control Number.* Once the book is published, one complimentary copy is sent to the Library of Congress.

There are no fees for participating in the PCN program. If you believe your work would be appropriate for libraries, request a PCN.

Participation sometimes results in orders for your book from sources who would not have known about it otherwise.

For more information, guidelines about what books qualify, instructions and PCN forms, visit their website.

Contact
Online
http://pcn.loc.gov

ISBN

What is an ISBN?

The International Standard Book Number (ISBN) is a 13-digit number that uniquely identifies your book as a specific title from a specific publisher (you).

Do I need to purchase an ISBN?

If you are selling your book on your own, you are not required to have an ISBN. However, if you plan to sell your book at online booksellers, in bookstores, or put it in libraries, then it is advisable to purchase a number.

Obtaining an ISBN

Visit **www.myidentifiers.com** to purchase your ISBN. The charge for a single number is $125.00 and a block of ten numbers is $400.00. After you've obtained your numerical ISBN, that number can be used to create a barcode for your back cover. A barcode is a graphic of vertical lines that encodes numerical information that can be scanned for sales or inventory (see the back of this book). The ISBN number is used to create the barcode, but the number and the barcode are two different things.

You can purchase both the number and barcode from the ISBN website—or you can purchase the number only, and for $25.00, have us make your barcode and place it on your back cover.

Contact

Write
ISBN Agency / R.R. Bowker
630 Central Avenue
New Providence, NJ 07974

Fax
908-219-0188

Online
http://www.myidentifiers.com

Selling your book

Marketing an unknown book by an unknown author can be a challenge, to say the least. Self-publishers generally do not have the contacts or clout to maneuver their books into major book selling avenues.

Another stumbling block is quantity vs. cost. Printing 25 books is considerably more expensive per book than printing 3,000 books. Therefore, there is less profit in selling books from a short run. Gambling on being able to sell 3,000 may not be a good bet either. The general consensus is to print a smaller first printing and hope to break even. Then go into a second printing. A second printing is less expensive because most of the setup costs have already been paid.

Who's your audience?

You know your book best—and selling your book yourself is the most practical way to get the book in front of your audience. Where do they shop? What do they like to do? How can you contact them?

Niche Market

Some authors deal with subject matter that has a small field of interest or niche market. These books are sometimes easier to sell because it is simpler to identify the market. For example, a book on rock hunting in Western Washington might be promoted with greater success sending out flyers or postcards to rock clubs than trying to work through a mass market bookstore.

Over the years, we have talked to many authors about their self-marketing efforts. The following pages list some techniques they have found helpful.

Marketing Tips

Edit and design stage

Apply for ISBN and/or LCCN:
(See pages 55 and 56.) Processing
can take 24 hours to 15 business
days depending upon price.

Consult a professional editor:
to help polish your book.

Create a logo: of your company
or use the title of your book as a logo.
Place on all correspondence and
publications for marketing
your book.

An order form: Placed on one of the last
pages, the order form is an excellent way
to maintain continuing sales of the book.

Explore all avenues

Before printing, brainstorm every
marketing method you can think
of—it may help you decide how
many books to print.

Back cover real estate

If a front cover draws in the reader,
the back cover is high-end real
estate to seal the deal.

What goes onto a back cover?

- **Category**: Your back cover should
  include a subject category at the top.
  This is a standardized heading used
  to help bookstores know where to
  place your book on their shelves.
  You can find a complete list at Book
  Industry Study Group, bisg.org.

- **Summary**: 100-200 word summary
  block to convey what's inside the
  book. You might use bullet points
  depending on the type of book.

- **Endorsements**: One or
  two reviews or cover blurbs
  are nice to have. Check out
  endorsementquest.com for tips
  and a sample endorsement
  request letter in an e-book by
  Gregory Kompes.

- **About the Author**: A 100 word or
  shorter description about you with
  a full-color head shot if you'd like.

Use the web

Get a website: Obtain a domain name for your company, book title or your name. Have a website created that showcases information about your book, including excerpts, an image of your book cover and a way for book orders to be submitted to you via the web. We recommend a company like American Author.com who can do all the work for you.

Create an email announcement: A simple email letter with an image of your book can be an effective promotional tool.

Online articles: The Internet is a great place to post information. You can reach hundreds of thousands of people by getting the word out about your book. You can submit your press release to places like prleap.com, pr.com or prweb.com, where it is possible your article may also be picked up by regular media.

Start a blog: These free online sites allow you to post information about the subject matter of your book, yourself, and /or upcoming events. One example is blogger.com.

In the news

Contact newspapers: Write a press release. This is usually a one-page article about you, your book and/or the subject matter. You want to hook a reporter's interest with a strong opening paragraph, and make them want to know more. To learn more, start at Paul Krupin's site directcontactpr.com.

Print advertising

Create promotional pieces: have a professional designer create items to assist in marketing such as: bookmarks with your web address or phone number, business cards, posters, flyers, brochures or extra printed covers.

Self-Publishing Help

Check out regional and national booksellers and small publishing groups for help in marketing, such as span.org or pma-online.org.

Get out there

Host an autograph party: Send out invitations and flyers in advance to advertise the release of your book.

Arrange speaking engagements: Offer to speak for free as an expert in your field and subject matter, and sell your book afterward.

Enter competitions

Enter writing or design competitions: Many organizations sponsor awards for excellence in writing and design. There is usually a fee involved per category:

- **Writer's Digest International Self-Publishing Book Awards:** click on Contests.

- **Independent Publisher Book Awards** (Ippy Awards): independentpublisher.com.

- **Ben Franklin Awards**: sponsored by PMA, The Independent Book Publisher's Association pma-online. org, click on Seminar and Awards.

Approach stores

Locally owned bookstores: They usually require a 40-50% discount. For a list of independent bookstores in your area or a specific zip code, go to Booksense.com.

Online bookstores and retailers: Though selling your book yourself has a larger profit margin, third party sales avenues are available. Depending on which way you go, anticipate a 40 to 60% discount of the retail price. Many bookstores prefer to buy from distributors such as Baker & Taylor or IPG. A distributor's fee is usually 50-60%.

- Join the Amazon.com Advantage Program. This is a direct way to send your book to customers all over the world.

- At BarnesandNoble.com, click on Publisher and Author Guidelines at the bottom of the web site for information about submitting your book.

Glossary

back matter—The pages after the main text of the book that contain the reference material, including: Appendix(es), Notes, Glossary, Bibliography, List of Contributors, Index(es) and Order Form (most often in that order).

barcode—A book barcode uses a sequence of vertical bars and spaces to represent the numbers of your ISBN.

bleed—A printed image that extends "off the page" is known as a bleed.

body text—The main text body of the book, separate from the display type such as headlines, subheadlines, chapter openings, etc.

CMYK—Initials designating Cyan (C), Magenta (M), Yellow (Y) and Black (K). Also known as the four process colors.

color management—A process using device profiles to interpret and translate color between devices.

color separations—The conversion of a color photograph or drawing into its component spectral colors: Cyan, Yellow, Magenta and Black (CMYK) with one screened negative produced per color.

copyright—A book is copyrighted when the author's name, date of copyright and the copyright symbol (©) or the word "copyright" appear on the copyright page (usually the first left-hand page after the title page).

crop marks—Small lines on the outer edges of a book cover that indicate the final trim size after it is bound.

registration—To print an image in correct relation to other images already printed on the same sheet.

formatting—The process of importing a raw text file into a page-layout program and designing the final book pages.

four-color process (full color) printing—The process of using four colors to print a single image, resulting in an image that looks full color to the naked eye. The ink colors used are: Cyan, Magenta, Yellow and Black.

front matter—The pages before the main text of the book that contain the Title page, Copyright page, Dedication, Foreword, Contents, Preface, Acknowledgment and Introduction (most often in that order.)

halftone—A process whereby a photograph is broken up into a pattern of dots of varying size. When printed, the dots of the image merge to the naked eye to give the impression of shades of gray.

header—Headers appear at the top of each page in the book (except chapter openings) and contain either the author name, book name or chapter name. They are designed to help the reader navigate around the book.

RIP—A postscript device that digitally images computer files.

ISBN—International Standard Book Number. A registration number obtained from R. R. Bowker that is used by bookstores to track and obtain titles.

Library of Congress Control Number—A registration number obtained from the Library of Congress that is used to distribute books intended for libraries.

leading—The space between lines of type.

mass market paperback—A small, non-illustrated, cheaper version of a book, typically printed on newsprint.

offset printing—The transfer of an inked image to paper through an intermediate, or blanket, cylinder.

negative (film)—A photographic image in which light values are reversed. Light is passed through this image onto a light-sensitive printing plate which is used on the press.

niche market—A focused, targetable portion of a market.

publishing (traditional)—Books that are printed, marketed and distributed by a publisher are said to be *published*. Writers receive a share of the profits. *See self-publishing.*

resolution—The quality of a digital output, as defined by the number of dots (pixels) per inch. The higher the number, the higher the quality.

sans-serif—A typeface without serifs (the short lines projecting from the top or bottom of the main stroke of a letter). *See serif.*

self-publishing—When an author chooses to print, market and distribute a book, paying all costs and keeping all rights and profits.

serif—The short lines that project from the top or bottom of the main stroke of a letter. *See sans-serif.*

signature—Folded book pages that are usually in groups of 8, 16 or sometimes 32. In the case of a 16–page signature, 8 pages are printed on each side of a large sheet of paper. The sheet is then folded into a signature. The signatures are bound together at the spine.

smyth sewn—A binding with threads sewn through the back fold of the signature, with threads carried also from signature to signature, linking them together, while permitting complete opening of the book to the back.

spine—The back of the book where the bound pages come together. Also the part of the book that is visible on bookshelves.

trapping—To anticipate mis-registration on the press that might result in an unintended white space where two printed colors are next to one another. One of the ink colors is made bigger (spread) or smaller (choke) to compensate for variables in printing.

trade paperback—A paperback book that is typically of better production quality, larger size and higher price than a mass-market edition.

trim size—The dimensions of the finished book, after it is printed, bound and trimmed on three sides.

WALT DISNEY
Bambi's Game

By Joan Phillips

Illustrated by Bill Langley
and Diana Wakeman

Dai Allred

A GOLDEN BOOK • NEW YORK

Western Publishing Company, Inc., Racine, Wisconsin 53404

Bambi likes to play.
He likes to play
with Thumper.
He likes to play
with Flower, too.

"Will you play with me?"
asks Bambi.

"Yes, I will play!"
says Flower.

"I will play, too!"
says Thumper.

"Can you do this?"
asks Bambi.
"Can you run like me?"

"Yes, I can!"
says Thumper.
"I can run like you,
Bambi!"

"I can run like you, too!"
says Flower.

"Can you do this?"
asks Bambi.
"Can you jump like me?"

"I can jump like you, too!"
says Flower.

"Can you run
this way
and that way?"
asks Bambi.

"Yes, I can!"
says Thumper.
"This game is fun!"
says Thumper.

Bambi and Thumper
do not hear Flower.

Bambi stops.
Thumper stops, too.
Bambi and Thumper
look back.
Flower is not there.

Where is Flower?

Bambi and Thumper
look for Flower.

They look behind a rock.
They look near a tree.
They look everywhere.
They cannot find Flower.

"Flower, where are you?"
call Bambi and Thumper.

Owl comes to help
find Flower.
The opossums come, too.
Lots of animals
come and help.

They look and look.
But they cannot
find Flower.

Then Thumper says,
"I hear something.
Listen."

"I hear something, too,"
says Bambi.
"I hear snoring!
I hear snoring
over there!

"COME OUT, FLOWER!"
shouts Bambi.
"WAKE UP, FLOWER!"
shouts Thumper.

Flower sits up.
"I was sleepy.

But now I am ready to play!"
he says.

"Let's play your game, Bambi,"
says Flower.
"Can you do this?
Can you walk like me?"

"Yes, I can!"
says Bambi.